Read-About® Math

A Garden Full of Sizes

By Simone T. Ribke

Consultant
Linda Bullock
Math Curriculum Specialist

Children's Press®
A Division of Scholastic Inc.
New York   Toronto   London   Auckland   Sydney
Mexico City   New Delhi   Hong Kong
Danbury, Connecticut

Designer: Herman Adler Design
Photo Researcher: Caroline Anderson
The photo on the cover shows a girl watering her garden.

Library of Congress Cataloging-in-Publication Data

Ribke, Simone T.
  A garden full of sizes / by Simone T. Ribke.—1st ed.
     p. cm. — (Rookie read-about math)
  Includes bibliographical references and index.
  ISBN 0-516-24432-9 (lib. bdg.)   0-516-25849-4 (pbk.)
  1. Size perception—Juvenile literature. 2. Size judgment—Juvenile
literature. I. Title. II. Series.
  BF299.S5R53 2004
  153.7'52—dc22
                                                2004005085

CHILDREN'S PRESS, and ROOKIE READ-ABOUT®,
and associated logos are trademarks and or registered trademarks
of Scholastic Library Publishing. SCHOLASTIC and associated logos
are trademarks and or registered trademarks of Scholastic Inc.
1 2 3 4 5 6 7 8 9 10 R 13 12 11 10 09 08 07 06 05 04

Our garden is full of nice surprises. There are many things in different sizes.

These people are planting flowers in a garden.

Tall shovel Short shovel

From the garden shed,
I must choose. Which
shovel is best to use?

This shovel is too **tall** for
me. This shovel is **short**.
It's perfect. Do you agree?

Large melons grow upon the ground.

Watermelons are big and round.

Tomatoes grow on vines.

Small tomatoes grow nice and round.

This butterfly is **bigger**
and easier to spot,

than the **smaller** ladybug
near the flowerpot.

The **biggest** strawberries
are just right for me. On
the ground, I see three.

Will more blueberries fit in my hand? Yes. Many of the **smallest** can.

Cucumber leaves grow
very **wide**. Weeds with
narrow leaves try to hide.

Pulling weeds is a fun chore. There are many. I look for more.

I like pumpkins. I'll plant five seeds. I'll give them all the water they need.

Pumpkin seeds are small.

Radish seeds are tiny.

I like radishes. I'll plant a lot. I'll plant them in the perfect spot.

I pick the peppers that are done. The **little** green ones need more sun.

Count the **big** red ripe ones that you see. How many are there? I count three.

There are three red peppers hiding here.

On these **thin** branches
the apples grow.

Then they fall by the **thick** trunk below.

I use a **long** green hose to
water the flowerbed.

Oh no! I see a **short** snake over by the shed.

This boy is cutting down a sunflower.

Many of the sunflowers are almost done. But we'll leave a few to grow in the sun.

Their **heavy** sunflower heads droop down.

Their petals are **light** and float to the ground.

The **big** scarecrow is built
of straw. Nothing frightens
him at all.

Nearby stands a **small**
garden gnome (NOME).
The flowerbed is his home.

Our garden is full of
nice surprises.

There are many things
in different sizes.

A family harvesting squash

This girl is proud of her beets.

Things grow **big** and **little**, **large** and **small**.

They grow **tall** and **short**, **thick** and **thin**.

Oh, what fun gardening has been!

Words You Know

long hose

short shovel

small tomatoes

30

thick trunk

thin branches

wide leaves

31

Index

About the Author

Simone T. Ribke is a writer and editor of children's books. Since earning a B.S. in Elementary Education, she has written a wide array of children's and professional educational materials, including work on a national math education program.

Photo Credits